ETA/Cuisen

ELEMENTARY

MATH

DICTIONARY

ETA
Cuisenaire

Vernon Hills, Illinois

ETA/Cuisenaire® Elementary Math Dictionary
ETA 42197
ISBN 978-0-7406-4822-9

ETA/Cuisenaire® • Vernon Hills, IL 60061-1862
800-445-5985 • www.etacuisenaire.com

Printed in China.

09 10 11 12 13 14 15   10 9 8

Introduction

The ETA/Cuisenaire® Elementary Math Dictionary is an essential guide to the mathematical language and concepts used in the United States school systems. It has been written with the young reader in mind, giving clear, simple, and concise definitions. Most definitions also include a colorful photo or diagram to assist with understanding. Worked examples offer further explanation. The words covered come from the 5 NCTM strands of the elementary mathematics curriculum.

This book is a handy, easy-to-use and easy-to-carry reference for all young students. Many everyday words take on a special meaning when we use them in mathematics. This can be confusing for students. Understanding mathematical language and symbols is an integral part of learning many mathematical concepts. The dictionary will also aid parents when they are assisting their children at home.

Useful reference charts include mathematical symbols, abbreviations, fraction tables, measurement tables, and Roman numerals.

Contents

abacus

- instrument made of rods and beads used for performing computations

acre

- a standard unit of measure used for measuring the area of large blocks of land

Fields are measured in acres.

acute angle

- an angle that measures between 0° and 90°

add

- to combine things

- to join together

addend

- any number used to get the sum or total

addition

- to combine two or more numbers to make one larger number

$$7 + 12 + 9 = 28$$

algebra

- a branch of mathematics that uses numbers, symbols, or letters to represent or express relationships

$$\blacklozenge \div 8 = 64$$

$$42 + \mathbf{y} = 52$$

algorithm

- a sequence of steps to get a desired result

A.M.

- stands for *ante meridiem*

- means the time from midnight to noon

sunrise

analog clock
- a clock that shows twelve-hour time

angle
- the amount of turning between two rays with a common endpoint

annual
- once every year

apex
- the vertex that is furthest from the base

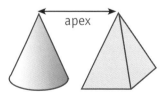

approximation
- very close, but not exact

200 is an approximation for 197.

arc
- a part of the circumference of a circle

area
- the size of a surface
- the space inside a boundary

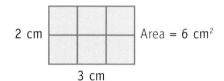

arithmetic
- an area of math that includes addition, subtraction, multiplication, and division of whole numbers, decimals, and fractions

array
- objects or numbers arranged in rows and columns

ascending order
- in order from smallest to largest

25, 85, 109, 153, 286

These numbers are written
in ascending order.

associative property
- two or more numbers can be added
(or multiplied) in any order

$(6 + 12) + 4 = 6 + (12 + 4)$

$(2 \times 9) \times 5 = 2 \times (9 \times 5)$

asymmetry
- having no lines of symmetry

This figure has asymmetry.

attribute
- a characteristic
of an object

- can be size
color, thickness,
length, etc.

autumn
- the season that follows summer

average
- is one score that tries to describe
or represent a group of scores

- to find the average, add all the
scores and divide by how many
scores there are

The average of 5, 9, 11, 7 and 8
is $(5 + 9 + 11 + 7 + 8) \div 5 = 8$

axis
- a scaled line that is a reference
line

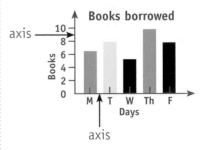

3

balance
- to have the same weight on either side

balance scale

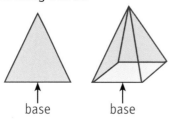

bar graph
- a graph that represents the data in a series of vertical columns or horizontal rows

bar notation
- a way of displaying repeating decimals

$$1\tfrac{1}{3} = 1.\overline{3}$$
$$2\tfrac{1}{66} = 2.01\overline{5}$$

base
- a line or surface on which something stands

base   base

base ten blocks
- blocks used to show place value

1,000   100   10   1

base number
- the basis of each place value column in a number system

10011010
Most computers calculate in binary. The base number for binary is 2.

base ten system
- a number system based on 10

bi-
- a prefix meaning "two"

billion
- a thousand million

$$1{,}000 \times 1{,}000{,}000 = 1{,}000{,}000{,}000$$

bisect
- to divide something into two equal parts

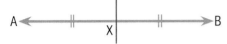

Line AB is bisected at X.

boundary
- a line around the outside edge

brackets
- symbols used to group things together

$$[9 \times 5] \times [7 - 3] = 56$$

breadth
- another name for width

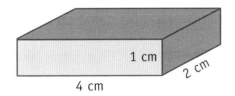

The breadth is 2 cm.

calculate
- to work something out

calculator
- a machine that works out mathematical equations

calendar
- a time map that tells us what day and month it is

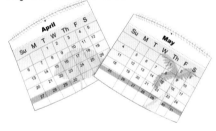

capacity
- how much something holds

- can be measured in millimeters (mL), liters (L), cups, or gallons

This container has a capacity of 2 liters.

cardinal numbers
- the numbers one, two, three, etc.

Celsius
- a temperature scale that is used to tell how hot or cold something is

- water boils at 100°C and freezes at 0°C

center
- the middle

- the midpoint of a circle

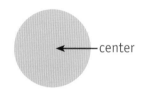
center

centimeter (cm)
- a measurement used for measuring length

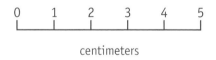
centimeters

cent (¢)
- a monetary unit worth one hundredth of a dollar

century
- 100 years

chance
- unpredictable and uncontrolled outcome

chord
- a straight line in a circle that goes from one point on the circumference to another point on the circumference but does not go through the center

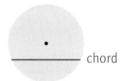

chord

circle
- a two-dimensional shape with 0 edges that has a center that is the same distance to any point on its round outer curve

circle graph
- drawn in a circle

- sectors are used to represent data

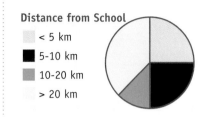

Distance from School
- < 5 km
- 5-10 km
- 10-20 km
- > 20 km

A circle graph is sometimes called a pie chart.

circumference
- the round outer curve of a circle

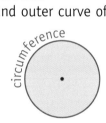

circumference

classify
- arrange in groups according to attributes

These flowers are classified according to color.

7

clockwise

- moving in the same direction as the hands of a clock

closed curve

- a curved line that is joined to its starting point

coefficient

- a number that multiplies a variable

color tiles

- manipulatives used for modeling important math concepts and develop basic arithmetic skills, logical thinking, algebra, and geometric thinking

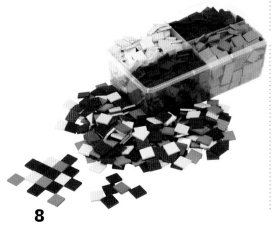

column

- a vertical arrangement of figures

$$93$$
$$42$$
$$7$$
$$19$$

common denominator

- a denominator that all fractions in a group can be changed to

One common denominator for $\frac{1}{2}, \frac{1}{3}, \frac{1}{4}$, is 12

$$\frac{1}{2}, = \frac{6}{12}, \frac{1}{3}, = \frac{4}{12}, \frac{1}{4} = \frac{3}{12}$$

common factor

- a whole number that divides two (or more) other numbers exactly

common multiple

- a multiple that is shared by two or more numbers

commutative property

- when adding (or multiplying) numbers it does not matter in what order they are added (or multiplied)

$$7 + 3 = 3 + 7$$

$$6 \times 8 = 8 \times 6$$

compass
- an instrument used to draw circles or arcs

complementary angles
- two angles whose sum is 90°

25° and 65° are complementary angles.

composite number
- a number which has more than two factors

10 has factors of 1, 2, 5 and 10. 10 is a composite number.

concentric circles
- two or more circles that have the same center

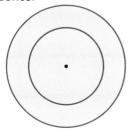

cone
- a three-dimensional object that has a circular base and one vertex

congruent
- having exactly the same size and shape

These triangles are congruent.

consecutive numbers
- numbers which follow one another

17, 18, 19, 20
are consecutive numbers.

converging lines
- two or more lines that meet at one point

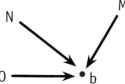

M, N, and O converge at Point b.

9

coordinates

- two numbers (or letters) which tell position on a grid

- horizontal number is written before the vertical number

- they are written in parentheses with a comma between

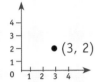

(3, 2) are the coordinates for the points on the grids.

corner
. - the point where lines meet the vertex

corresponding angles
- angles that are the same position made by a line cutting through two or more parallel lines

counterclockwise
- moving the opposite direction as the hands on the clock

cross-section
- what you see when an object is cut through

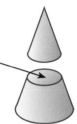

cube
- a three-dimensional object which has six identical square faces

cubed number
- to cube a number is to use it as a factor three times

$(7^3 = 343)$ means 7 x 7 x 7 = 343

7^3 is read "seven cubed."

343 is called a "perfect cube."

cubic measure

- measurement used to determine volume

- measurements can be cubic centimeter (cm³), cubic meter (m³), cubic inches (in³), etc.

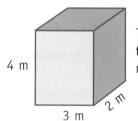

The volume of this box is 24 m³.

4 m

3 m

2 m

Cuisenaire® Rods

- manipulatives used to reinforce key math topics such as addition, subtraction, multiplication, division, measurement, area, and perimeter

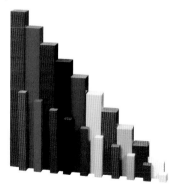

cylinder

- a three-dimensional object that has two circular ends and a curved surface joining the ends

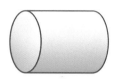

11

data

- a collection of information such as facts or measurements

What are the most popular fruits eaten by your friends?

This is the data.

Fruit	Number of people
orange	3
apple	4
plum	6
peach	10
grape	9
watermelon	12

date

- tells us what day, month, and year it is

day

- twenty-four hours which start and end at midnight

deca-

- a prefix meaning ten

> decagon – a 10-sided figure
> decade – 10 years

decade

- 10 years

decagon

- a polygon with 10 straight sides

decimal

- based on the number 10

decimal fraction

- a fraction with a denominator of power 10 written with a decimal point

The decimal fraction 0.65 is equal to $\frac{65}{100}$.

decimeter (dm)

- one tenth of a meter

decrease

- to make smaller

The sand pile has decreased in size.

deduct

-to take away from

> Deduct $4 from your pay.
> (Take $4 away from your pay.)

degree (°)

- a measurement used to measure angles

- also a measurement used to measure temperature

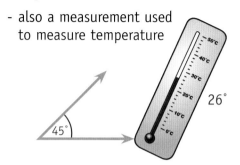

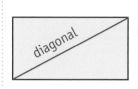

26°

45°

denominator

- the bottom number in a fraction

$\frac{1}{4}$ 4 is the denominator.

density

- the mass per unit of volume

descending order

- in order from largest to smallest

204, 189, 132, 87, 31, 13
These numbers are written in descending order.

diagonal

- a straight line that is drawn inside a shape from one vertex to another

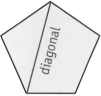

diagonal

diagonal

diagram

- a picture used to describe something

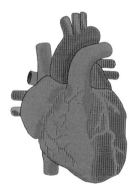

a diagram of a heart

diameter

- a straight line drawn from one point on the circumference to a circle through the center to another point on the circumference of the circle

diameter

diamond

- another name for a rhombus

die (plural is dice)

- a numbered cube that is often used in games

difference

- the amount by which one number is bigger or smaller than another number

The difference between
7 and 11 is 4.

digit

- one of our numerals

0, 1, 2, 3, 4, 5, 6, 7, 8, 9
are the digits we use.

digital clock

- a clock that has no hands and uses numerals to show time

dimension

- a measure of size

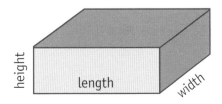

height

length

width

Length, height, and width are dimensions.

direction
- the way something is placed or pointing

discount
- a reduction in money

The discount is $2.

displacement
- how much water rises when an object is placed in it

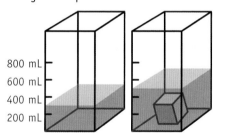

The displacement is 200 mL.

distance
- the length between two points

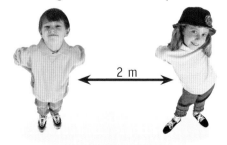

2 m

The distance between the children is 2 meters.

distributive property

$3 \times 8 + 3 \times 4 = 3 \times (8 + 4)$

$2 \times 7 + 9 \times 7 = (2 \times 9) \times 7$

divide
- to place numbers or objects into groups

These 12 feathers are divided into 3 groups.

dividend
- the amount to be divided

$$36 \div 9 = 4$$
36 is the dividend.

division
- the act of dividing into groups

$$6 \overline{)72} \quad 12$$

divisor
- the number used to divide by

$$36 \div 9 = 4$$
9 is the divisor.

15

dodecagon

- a polygon with
  12 straight sides

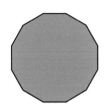

dominoes

- rectangular tiles with one face divided into two parts marked with dots
- used to play games

dot paper

- paper marked with a regular dot pattern
- can be square or isometric

square dots   isometric dots

double

- make twice as many or twice as big

Double 6 is 12.
Double 3 kg is 6 kg.

dozen

- 12 things together

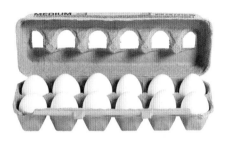

one dozen eggs

edge
- where two faces meet

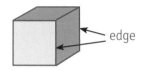

element
-member of a set

ellipse
- a curved shape like a squashed circle

endpoint
- a point marking the end of a line segment

enlarge
- to make something bigger

The orange has been enlarged.

equal
- exactly the same in value or size

6 + 3 is equal to 9.

(6 + 3 = 9)

100 cm is equal to 1 m.

(100 cm = 1 m)

equation
- a mathematical expression where one part is equal to another part

- an equal sign (=) is used

$8 \times 2 = 12 + 4$

equilateral triangle
- a triangle that has three equal sides

- its angles are all 60°

equivalent
- having the same value

equivalent fractions

- fractions which have the same value

$\frac{1}{2}$ and $\frac{5}{10}$ are equivalent fractions.

estimate

- to make a close guess

- it is never an exact answer

$$215 + 683$$
900 is the estimation.

evaluate

- to work out the value

☺ − 5 = 9 Evaluate for ☺.
☺ = 14

even number

- a whole number that can be divided exactly by 2

- ends in 0, 2, 4, 6, or 8

112 is an even number.
221 is not an even number.

expanded notation

- writing a number to show the value of each digit

$27,691 = 20,000 + 7,000 + 600 + 90 + 1$

exponent

- a small number, placed to the upper right of the base, showing the number of times the base number is multiplied by itself

$$8^2 = 64$$
In 8^2, 2 is the exponent.

expression

- a string of numbers and symbols connected by operation signs

$76 \div 4$ is an expression.
$67 \times$ ■ $- 42 \div 3$ is also an expression.

face
- a flat surface of a solid object

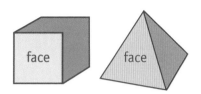

factor
- a whole number that is divides exactly into another number

12 ÷ 4 = 3   so 4 is a factor of 12.
Other factors of 12 are
1, 2, 3, 6, 12.

Fibonacci sequence
- sequence of numbers where the first two terms are 1 and every term after is found by adding the previous two terms

1, 1, 2, 3, 5, 8, 13, 21, 34, 55 ...

figurate numbers
- numbers that can be represented in a geometrical shape, including square, triangular, and pentagonal numbers

finite number
- a definite number

- can be counted

> There are a finite number of children in your school.
> There are a finite number of people in the world.

first
- comes before anything else

flip
- turn something over on one edge

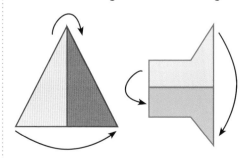

F

foot (ft)
- standard unit of measure
  equivalent to 12 inches

formula
- a rule

- shows how to work something out

The formula for finding the area
of a rectangle is $A = l \times w$.

A stands for area, l for length, and
w for width.

5 m

2 m

$A = l \times w$
$= 5 \times 2$
$= 10 \text{ m}^2$

fraction
- a part of a group or of a whole
  number

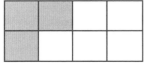

One car is circled. $\dfrac{1}{5}$

$\dfrac{3}{8}$

fraction bar
- line that separates the numerator
  and the denominator

$$\frac{2}{5} \longleftarrow \text{fraction bar}$$

frequency
- how often something happens

1	5	3	2
5	2	3	3
2	3	6	1
3	1	4	3

In this table:

3 has a frequency of 6.

4 has a frequency of 1.

function
- a mathematical relationship
  between two values

gallon (gal)
- standard unit of capacity used for measuring liquids
- 128 fluid ounces

geoboard
- a studded base board
- rubber bands are stretched around the studs to make shapes

geometry
- a part of mathematics which deals with two-dimensional and three-dimensional space
- shapes, objects, size, position

GeoTool® Compass
- a compass and protractor that has adjustable radii

googol
- the number written as 1 followed by 100 zeros

$$10^{100}$$

gram (g)
- a measurement used for weight
- 1,000 grams = 1 kilogram

These strawberries weigh 250 g.

graph
- a diagram that shows a collection of data

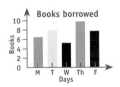

bar graph

picture graph

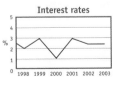

line graph

pie graph

greater than
- the symbol >

  7 > 2 tells us that 7 is greater than 2.

greatest common factor
- the biggest number that will divide two or more numbers exactly

gross
- twelve dozen or 144

gross mass
- the total mass; contents and container

grouping
- placing objects into groups that are equal in size

15 beetles are placed into 3 groups.

hand span
- the distance between the tips of the thumb and little finger on an outstretched hand

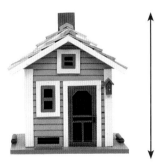

height
- the vertical distance from top to bottom

hemisphere
- half of a sphere

heptagon
- a polygon that has 7 straight sides

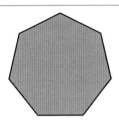

hexagon
- a polygon that has six straight sides

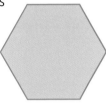

Hindu-Arabic number system
- was developed from the Hindus and Arabs

- uses numerals that include zero as a place keeper

  0, 1, 2, 3, 4, 5, 6, 7, 8, 9

histogram
- a bar graph representing frequency distribution

H

horizontal
- parallel to the horizon
- side to side

← horizon

This photo shows the horizon.

hour (hr)
- 60 minutes

The amount of time between 1 o'clock and 2 o'clock is one hour.

hundredth
- one part out of 100 parts

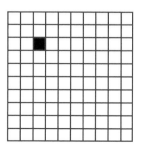

hypotenuse
- the side opposite the right angle of a right triangle

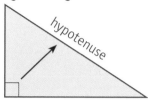

hypotenuse

improper fraction
- a fraction which has a numerator bigger than its denominator

  $\frac{3}{2}$ and $\frac{10}{7}$ are improper fractions.

inch (in.)
- standard unit of measure

- equivalent to about 2.54 centimeters

increase
- to make something bigger

The amount of water in the bowl will increase.

inequality
- quantities that are not equal in size or value

infinite
- never ending

- has no boundaries

  The set of even numbers is an infinite set. There is no last number.

infinity (∞)
- the state of being endless

- cannot be given an exact value

integer
- a whole number and their opposites

- can be positive, negative, or zero.

  -7 is an integer.
  315 is an integer.

intersect
- to cut across each other

This sign is used when roads intersect.

These are intersecting lines.

interval

- a part of a straight line

- has definite starting and ending points

A ●━━━━━━━━━━━━━━● B

The interval AB is 5 cm long.

inverse operations

- operations that undo each other

- addition and subtraction are inverse, as are multiplication and division

irrational number

- a real number than can be written as a nonrepeating or nonterminating decimal but not as a fraction

π and $\sqrt{2}$ are irrational numbers.

irregular polygon

- sides are not equal in length

- angles are not equal in size

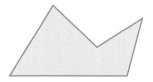

an irregular pentagon

isometric dot paper

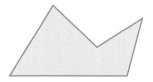

isosceles triangle

- has two equal sides

- the angles opposite the equal sides are also equal

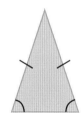

key
- the information needed to read a picture graph or diagram

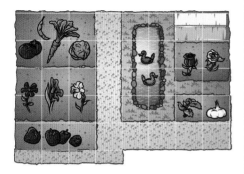

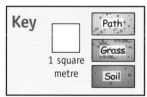

kilo-
- a prefix meaning one thousand

kilogram (kg)
- a measure of mass

This dog weighs 7 kg.

kiloliter (kL)
- a measure for large amounts of fluid

An Olympic pool holds 1,000 kL of water.

kilometer (km)
- a measure for long distances

The length of a road is measured in kilometers.

kite
- a 4-sided two-dimensional figure

- has two pairs of equal adjacent sides

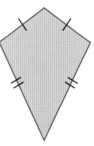

27

L

leap year
- has 366 days

- in a leap year February has 29 days

- happens every 4th year

2024 is a leap year.
2028 is the next leap year.

February						
Sun	Mon	Tues	Wed	Thur	Fri	Sat
	1	2	3	4	5	6
7	8	9	10	11	12	13
14	15	16	17	18	19	20
21	22	23	24	25	26	27
28	29					

This calendar shows February
in a leap year.

least
- the smallest

The small bottle
holds the least oil.

least common denominator
- the smallest number which the
  denominators will divide exactly

least common multiple
- the smallest number that is a
  multiple of two or more other
  numbers

length
- the distance from end to end

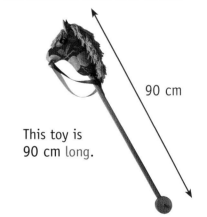

90 cm

This toy is
90 cm long.

less than
- the symbol <

13 < 29 tells us that
13 is less than 29.

line graph
- uses axes and lines to show data

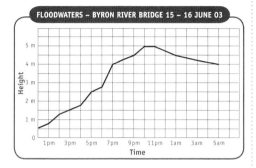

FLOODWATERS – BYRON RIVER BRIDGE 15 – 16 JUNE 03

lines
- parallel lines are straight lines that never meet no matter how far they are drawn
- perpendicular lines meet at right angles

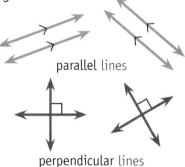

parallel lines

perpendicular lines

line symmetry
- a shape has line symmetry if both halves match exactly when it is folded on the line of symmetry
- line of symmetry is also called the axis of symmetry

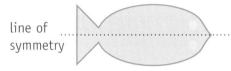

line of symmetry

liter (L)
- a measure used for liquids

This bottle can measure 4 L.

magic square
- a square filled with numbers
- the numbers in each row, each column, and each diagonal all have the same sum

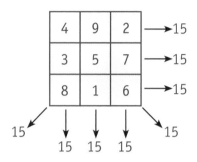

map
- a diagram of a country or place that shows its position in the world
- always drawn to scale

mass
- matter in an object
- measured in grams and kilograms

maximum
- the most

mean
- another name for average

measure
- to work out the size or amount of an object or distance

median
- the middle score (or scores) when a set of scores are written in order of size

Scores: 3, 3, 5, ⑦, 8, 11, 12
Median: 7

meter (m)
- a measure used for length or distance

Running races are measured in meters.

metric system
- a system of measures based on the decimal system
- centimeter, meter, milliliter, liter, and gram are some of the measurements used in the metric system

mile (mi)
- standard unit of measure for distance
- equivalent to 5,280 feet and 1,760 yards

millennium
- a thousand years

> All the years from 2000 to 2999 make a millennium.

milli-
- a prefix meaning one-thousandth

milliliter (mL)
- a measure used for small amounts of liquid

Medicines are measured in milliliters.

millimeter (mm)
- a measure used for small lengths

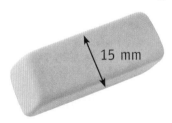

15 mm

This eraser is 15 millimeters wide.

million
- a thousand thousands
- 1,000,000

M

minimum
- the least amount

The minimum temperature for the last 24 hours was 0°C.

minus
- another word for subtract

- to take away

24 minus 7 is 17.

24 − 7 = 17

minute
- a measure of time

- 60 seconds is one minute

minute hand
- the long hand on a clock that tells the minutes

- it moves once around the clock face every hour

minute hand

mirror image
- an image which reflects another image exactly

mixed number
- has a whole number and a proper fraction

$6\frac{1}{2}$ is a mixed number.

whole number   proper fraction

mode
- a score that occurs most often in a set of scores

Scores: 4, 5, 7, 7, 8, 4, 7, 6, 5
Mode: 7

model
- a small copy that shows what something looks like

a model train engine

month
- a measure of time
- there are 12 months in a year

multiple
- the product of two or more factors

7 x 8 = 56
56 is a multiple of 7 and also of 8

multiplicand
- the number being multiplied by another

6 x 9 = 54
6 is the multiplicand.

multiplication
- the total in a number of groups or rows

5 x 4 = 20

4 x 6 = 24

multiplier
- the number that is doing the multiplying

6 x 9 = 54
9 is the multiplier.

natural number
- a counting number from one to infinity (1, 2, 3, ...)

negative number
- a number less than zero

- written with a minus sign in front of it

-4 -3 -2 -1 0 1 2 3 4

negative numbers   positive numbers

net
- a flat pattern that can be used to make a three-dimensional object

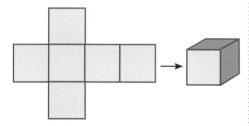

net of a cube

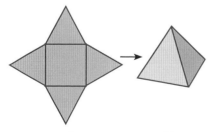

net of a square pyramid

net mass
- the mass of the contents not including the packaging

nonagon
- a polygon with 9 straight sides

notation
- a special way of writing numbers or mathematical expressions

Index notation uses indices
to write numbers.
7^3 means 7 x 7 x 7

number line
- a line used to show the position of a number

-3 -2 -1 0 1 2 3

A number line can help with addition.

number sentence

- a sentence written using numerals and signs

- shows a relationship between numbers

$$(7 - 4) \times 8 = 24$$

is a number sentence.

numeral

- a symbol (or group of symbols) that stands for a number

0, 1, 2, 3, 4, 5, 6, 7, 8, 9
are the numerals we use in
the metric system.

numerator

- the top number in a fraction

- tells us how many parts of a whole we have

$\dfrac{3}{8}$ 3 is the numerator.

It tells us that we have
3 eighths.

oblique
- slanting

This is an oblique line.

oblong
- another name for a rectangle that is not a square

obtuse angle
- an angle larger than a right angle but smaller than a straight angle
- measures between 90° and 180°

octagon
- a polygon that has eight straight sides

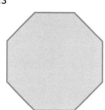

odd number
- a number that cannot be divided exactly by two
- ends in 1, 3, 4, 5, 7, or 9

15, 69, 441
are all odd numbers.

odometer
- an instrument that measures distance traveled (as in a car)

operation
- one of the four methods of solving mathematical problems (+, −, x, ÷)

addition 5 + 7 + 9
subtraction 259 − 165
multiplication 28 x 36
division 267 ÷ 13

ordered pair
- a pair of numbers that locates a point in a coordinate plane
- (1, 2) is an ordered pair

ordering

- placing a group in order according to a given instruction, eg. size, weight, length, etc.

These children are ordered according to height.

8, 23, 41, 88, 107
These numbers are in ascending order.

order of operations

- work everything inside parentheses first

- then work all the x and ÷ left to right

- finally work all the + and − from left to right

$7 \times (8 + 3) - 35 \div 7$ $= 7 \times 11 - 35 \div 7$
$= 77 - 5$
$= 72$

ordinal number

- tells position

- 1st, 2nd, 3rd, 4th, 5th, etc.

ounce (oz)

- a standard unit for measuring weight

outlier

- a value far away from most of the rest in a set of data

oval

- a closed curve that looks like a squashed circle

P

pair
- two together
- to make twos

a pair of shoes

palindrome
- reads the same backwards and forwards

676   1380831

palindromic numbers

parallel lines
- two or more lines that will never meet no matter how far they are drawn

parallel lines

parallelogram
- a special quadrilateral
- opposite sides are parallel
- opposite angles are equal

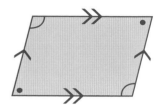

pattern
- numbers or objects that are arranged following a rule

1, 6, 11, 16, 21, 26
The rule is to add 5.

pattern blocks
- blocks that can be used to form patterns
- they are in many shapes

PentaBlocks®
- geometric shapes used to create repeating patterns, symmetry, congruence, ratios, and fractions

pentagon
- a polygon that has 5 straight sides

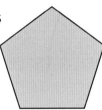

pentominoes
- manipulative used for studying geometry, fractions, and area

- each piece is constructed from five squares

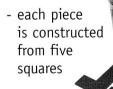

percent (%)
- out of 100

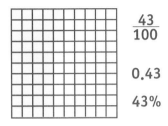

$$\frac{43}{100}$$

0.43

43%

perimeter
- the distance around the outside of a shape

- add the lengths of all the sides

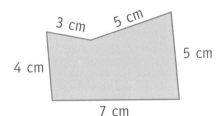

3 cm   5 cm

4 cm

5 cm

7 cm

P = 4 cm + 3 cm + 5 cm + 5 cm + 7 cm

P = 24 cm

P

perpendicular lines

- lines that intersect at right angles

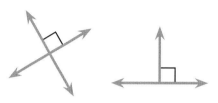

perpendicular lines

perspective

- the appearance of objects affected by size and position

This photograph of street lights shows perspective.

pi (π)

- the ration of the circumference of a circle to its diameter

- does not have an exact decimal value (≈ 3.14)

picture graph

- uses pictures to represent data

- a key is used to interpret the pictures

Taxis seen on the way home	
Adam	
Bill	
Martha	

Key = 2 taxis

pint (pt)

- a standard unit for measuring capacity

- equivalent to 16 fluid ounces

place value

- value according to place in a number

7,382

The place value of the 3 is *hundreds* because it is in the hundreds place.
The value of the 3 is 300.

plan
- a diagram that shows a view of the whole structure

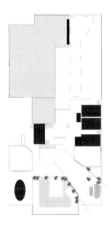

a floor plan of a house

plane shape
- a two-dimensional shape that is drawn on a flat surface

These are plane shapes.

Platonic solids
- five regular polyhedra

- faces are regular polygons

- are named after Plato

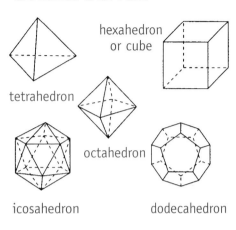

tetrahedron

hexahedron or cube

octahedron

icosahedron

dodecahedron

plus (+)
- another word for add

P.M.
- stands for *post meridiem*

- means the time from noon to midnight

41

P

polygon

- a two-dimensional shape with three or more sides and angles

- name comes from Greek words meaning "many" and "angle"

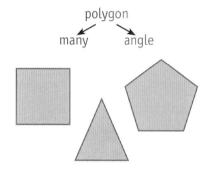

These are all polygons.

polyhedron

- a solid object that has polygons as faces

- a regular polyhedron has all congruent faces

- pyramids and prisms are polyhedrons

polyomino

- a shape made from squares which are all the same size

Some polyominos are:

domino (2 squares)

triomino (3 squares)

tetromino (4 squares)

pentomino (5 squares)

population

- a whole set of individuals, items, or data from which a statistical sample is drawn

position
- where something is placed in relation to the things around it

The juice is in the glass.
The strawberries are on the plate.
The glass is behind the cup.

positive number
- a number greater than zero

pound (lb)
- a standard unit for measuring weight

power of
- the power of a number is shown by an index number

- to find a power, a number is multiplied by itself a number of times

8^3 is 8 to the power of three.
(8 x 8 x 8)
2^7 is 2 to the power of seven.
(2 x 2 x 2 x 2 x 2 x 2 x 2)

prime factor
- a factor that is a prime number

The prime factors of 12 are
2 x 2 x 3.

prime factorization
- to write a number as a product of prime factors
(e.g. 36 = 2 x 2 x 3 x 3)

prime number
- a number that has only two factors: itself and one

13 is a prime number.
Its only factors are 1 and 13.

prism
- a three-dimensional object

- it has two identical ends which give the prism its name

- all other faces are rectangles

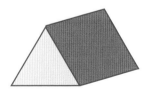

a triangular prism

P

probability

- the chances of something happening

- words such as possible, certain, unlikely, sure, impossible, and most likely are used for probability

It is certain to rain this year.

problem

- a question that is answered by using mathematics

- some problems use words and some only use numbers

a number problem
98 x 12

Jo had 50 cherries and ate 34 of them. How many are left?

product

- the answer when two or more numbers are multiplied

7 x 3 = 21
21 is the product.

15 x 3 x 7 = 315
315 is the product.

proper fraction

- the numerator is smaller than the denominator

$\frac{1}{3}, \frac{2}{5}, \frac{8}{10}, \frac{21}{37}$
are all proper fractions.

protractor

- an instrument used to measure or draw angles

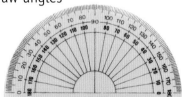

pyramid

- a three-dimensional object

- it has one base which gives the pyramid its name

- all other faces are triangles

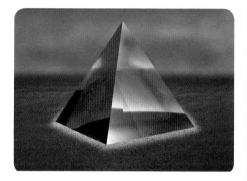

Pythagorean theorem

- the sum of the squares of the lengths of the sides of a right triangle is equal to the square of the length of the hypotenuse

quadrant
- any of the four areas into which a plane is divided by the reference axes in a Cartesian coordinate system, designated first, second, third, and fourth, counting counterclockwise from the area in which both coordinates are positive

quadrilateral
- a polygon with four straight sides

qualitative data
- data categories like food, clothes, or hobbies

quantitative data
- data that can be counted or measured

quart (qt)
- a standard unit for measuring capacity

- equivalent to 32 fluid ounces

quarter
- one of four equal parts of a group or object

$\frac{1}{4}$ of the square

$\frac{1}{4}$ of the wrenches

quotient
- the answer when one number is divided by another

$$36 \div 9 = 4$$
4 is the quotient.

radius
- the distance from the center of a circle to the circumference

random
- without any pattern or plan

choosing at random

range
- the difference between the lowest and highest scores in a group of scores

3, 6, 9, 1, 9, 4, 3, 5, 7
The range of this group of scores is 8 (9 − 1).

ratio (:)
- compares two or more like quantities

The ratio of cats to dogs is 1:3.

rational number
- a real number that can be written as a fraction, a repeating decimal, or an integer

ray
- part of a straight line
- it has a definite starting point but no end

ray

47

rectangle
- a special quadrilateral
- all angles are right angles
- opposite sides are equal

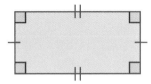

reduce
- to make smaller

reflection
- a shape or object as seen in a mirror

reflex angle
- an angle that measures between 180° and 360°

regular polygon
- a polygon that has all sides equal
- it also has all angles equal

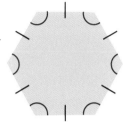

This is a regular hexagon.

remainder
- the amount left over when one number cannot be divided exactly by another

$$17 \div 7 = 2 \text{ with } 3 \text{ left over.}$$
$$3 \text{ is the remainder.}$$

repeating decimal
- some numbers in the decimal keep repeating
- the repeating numbers have bars over them
- a never-ending decimal

$$\frac{1}{3} = 0.33333333333 \ldots$$
$$= 0.\overline{3} \ldots$$
$$\frac{3}{11} = 0.272727272727 \ldots$$
$$= 0.\overline{27} \ldots$$

revolution
- an angle that measures 360°

- a complete turn through 4 right
  angles

rhombus
- a special quadrilateral

- all sides are equal

- opposite sides are parallel

- opposite angles are equal

right angle
- an angle that measures 90°

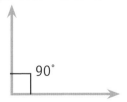

right triangle
- a triangle that has one right angle

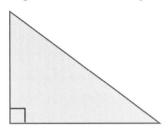

Roman numerals
- a number system used by the
  ancient Romans

- I, V, X, L, C, D, M are the symbols
  used

$$MDCLXX = 1,670$$

rotation
- to turn an object

rotational symmetry
- when a shape looks the same in
  different positions as it is turned
  at a fixed point, it has rotational
  symmetry

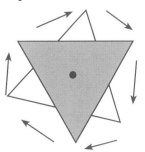

rounding
- giving an approximate answer

Round to the nearest hundred.

$4,539 \approx 4,500$

(because 3 lets the hundreds
numeral remain unchanged)

$7,264 \approx 7,300$

(because the numeral 6 tells us to
+1 to the hundreds numeral)

row
- numbers or objects in a horizontal
line

2, 4, 6, 8, 10, 12

A row of even numbers.

A row of paper people.

rule
- an instruction that applies to a
sequence of numbers or a pattern

1, 2, 4, 8, 16

Rule: double to get the new term.

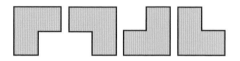

Rule: turn shape 90° clockwise.

sample
- a section or part of a whole group

scale
- the ratio of the lengths shown to the real length it represents

Scale 1:100

The picture is 4 cm high so the giraffe is really 400 cm high.

scale drawing
- enlarging or decreasing the size of a drawing to a given scale

scalene triangle
- a triangle that has sides of different lengths

- the angles are different sizes

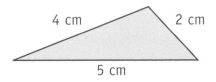

4 cm   2 cm

5 cm

scales
- instruments used to weight objects

- also used to compare masses

scientific notation
- a way of writing very large or very small numbers using a number between 1 and 10 multiplied by a power of ten

$$4{,}370 = 4.37 \times 10^3$$
$$0.000009 = 9 \times 10^{-6}$$

season
- there are 4 seasons in a year: spring, summer, autumn, winter

second (sec)
- a very short measure of time

- there are 60 seconds in 1 minute

section
- a part of a whole

These are sections of mandarin.

sector
- a part of a circle bounded by two radii and an arc

segment
- a part of a circle bounded by a chord and an arc

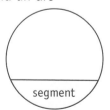

semicircle
- half of a circle

sequence
- a list of numbers or objects which are in a special order

1, 1, 2, 3, 5, 8, 13 ...

This is a special sequence called the Fibonacci sequence.

set
- a collection of objects or numbers

- each member is called an element of the set

Spring, Summer, Autumn, Winter
This is the set of seasons in a year.

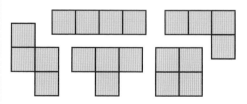

This is the set of tetrominos.

set square
- an instrument shaped like a right triangle
- can be used to draw right angles
- can be used to draw parallel lines

side
- one of the lines that form a two-dimensional shape

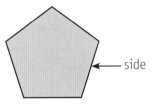

A pentagon has 5 sides.

side view
- what you see when you look at an object from the side

sign
- a symbol used instead of words

$$+, \%, >, \pi, \sqrt{}, \approx$$

These are some signs we use in math.

similar
- they have the same shape, but are different sizes

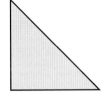

size
- how big an object is

A lion is a large cat.

skip counting
- to count on or to count back in groups of the same size

> 10, 15, 20, 25, 30
> This is skip counting on in groups of 5.

> 20, 17, 14, 11, 8
> This is skip counting back in groups of 3.

slide
- to move a shape without lifting it
- it has no change in direction or placement of features

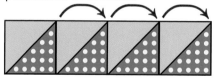

Snap Cubes®
- manipulatives used for modeling number concepts and other spatial reasoning tasks

solid
- an object that has three dimensions: length, height, and width

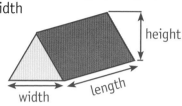

sort
- to place things into like groups

These are sorted into fruits and vegetables.

fruits

vegetables

speed
- how fast something is moving

The speed of the rollercoaster is
45 miles per hour.

sphere
- a three-dimensional
  object shaped
  like a ball

spinner
- a disc that can be spun to show
  numbers or colors at random

spiral
- an open curve that winds around
- can be endless

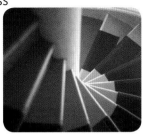

spring
- the season that follows winter

square
- a polygon with
  four equal sides
  and four right
  angles

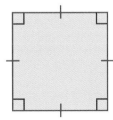

square measure

- the measurement used when finding area

- includes cm^2, m^2, ft^2

square number

- when a number is multiplied by itself the answer is a square number

- a square number can always form a square pattern

$$7 \times 7 = 49$$
49 is a square number.

$7 \times 7 =$

square root ($\sqrt{\ }$)

- of a given number is the number that when multiplied by itself, makes the given number

$\sqrt{81} = 9$ because $9 \times 9 = 81$

statistics

- facts and figures presented in numbers

- information is collected by survey

straight angle

- an angle which looks like a straight line

- always measures $180°$

straight line

- the shortest distance between two points

The shortest distance between Smelly Swamp and Golden Sands is the line AB.

strategy
- a method for working something out

73 x 4

A good strategy for multiplying by 4 is to double and double again.

73 doubled = 146 and
146 doubled = 292
so 73 x 4 = 292

subtract
- to take one number away from another

12 – 7 = 5

sum
- the total when numbers are added

3 + 5 + 9 = 17
17 is the sum of 3, 5, and 9.

summer
- the season that follows spring

supplementary angles
- two angles that total 180°
- together they make a straight angle

120° 60°

60° and 120° are
supplementary angles.

77° 103°

103° and 77° are
supplementary angles.

surface
- the top or outside layer of an object
- it can be flat or curved

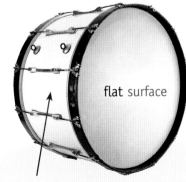

flat surface

curved surface

surface area
- the total area of all the surfaces of a three-dimensional object

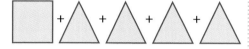

The surface area of this square pyramid is the area of the square base plus the areas of the four triangular sides.

survey
- to collect facts or data about a topic

Sport	Tally	Total
Tennis	||||| ||||| ||||| ||||| ||	22
Soccer	||||| ||||| |||||	15
Basketball	||||| ||||| ||||| |||	18
Football	||||| ||||| ||||| ||||||||	24
Golf	||||| ||||| ||||| |||||		21

100 people were surveyed about their favorite sport.

symbol
- a sign or letter used instead of words

+ (plus), π (pi), √ (square root), ≠ (is not equal to)

symmetry
- when one half of a shape is a reflection of the other half

- when folded on an axis of symmetry the two halves fit exactly on top of each other

axis of symmetry

table

- numbers or quantities arranged in rows and columns

SNACK AROUND THE WORLD

	Hotdog	Coffee	Hamburger
New York	$2.50	$1.75	$3.10
Hong Kong	$4.25	$3.95	$6.40
Vancouver	$3.35	$2.85	$4.50
London	£3.00	£4.00	£5.10
Singapore	$3.35	$1.95	$3.90

tables

- a short name for all the multiplication facts

take away

- to find the difference between two things or numbers

$$17 \text{ take away } 9$$
$$17 - 9 = 8$$

tally

- to count how many there are

tally marks

- marks used to help when counting a large number

- they are drawn in bundles of five

$$\text{⫻⫻ ⫻⫻ ⫻⫻ ⫻⫻ ⫻⫻ ⏐⏐} = 27$$

tangram

- a traditional Chinese puzzle

- a square cut into one parallelogram, one square, and five triangles

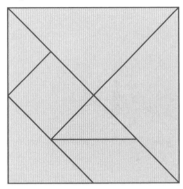

temperature

- how hot or cold a thing is

The temperature is hot.

The temperature is cold.

59

term
- one of the parts (elements) of a sequence

4, 8, 12, 16, 20

8 is the second term in this sequence.

tessellation
- a pattern made of identical shapes

- the shapes fit together without any gaps

-the shapes do not overlap

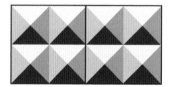

This tessellating pattern is made with triangles.

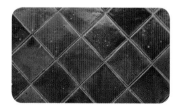

This tessellating pattern is made with squares.

tetrahedron
- a polygon that has four faces

thermometer
- an instrument used to measure temperature

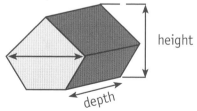

three-dimensional
- an object that has height, width, and depth

height

depth

time
- the space between one event and the next

- the space taken by an action

It takes Tom 17 minutes
to eat breakfast.

time line
- a diagram used to show the length of time between things happening

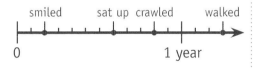

times
- another word for multiply

3 times 8 is the same as 3 x 8

timetable
- a table where times are organized for when things happen

- examples are bus timetables, school timetables, TV timetables

ton (T)
- a standard unit of mass

- equivalent to 2,000 pounds

tonne (t)
- a unit of mass

- equivalent to 1,000 kilograms

An elephant can weigh 7 tonnes.

total
- add all the numbers to find the total

5 + 19 + 32 + 6 + 18 = 80
80 is the total.

T

trading
- changing a number into smaller or bigger parts

transformation
- moving a shape so that the shape does not change but it is in a different position
- flip, slide, or turn can be used for a transformation

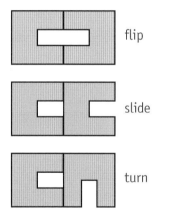

flip

slide

turn

translation
- to move an item in any direction without rotation it

trapezoid
- a special quadrilateral
- one pair of opposite sides are parallel

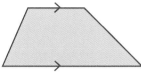

triangle
- a polygon with three straight sides

triangular number
- a number that can make a triangular dot pattern

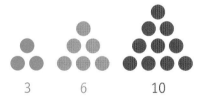

3   6   10

3, 6, and 10 are triangular numbers.

trundle wheel
- an instrument used to measure lengths

turn
- to rotate about a point

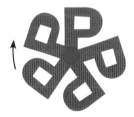

P is turning.

two-dimensional
- a shape that only has two dimensions; length and width (height)

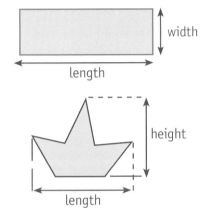

unequal (≠)
- not equal to

$$7 + 4 \neq 5 + 8$$

unit
- a unit is one

- units are recorded in the ONES column

Hundreds	Tens	Ones
	3	7

3 tens and 7 units

units of measurement
- standard units used for comparison

Units of length are millimeter, centimeter, meter, kilometer.

Units of time are second, minute, hour, day, week, month, year, decade.

value
- what something is worth

variable
- a quantity which is represented by a symbol and can have different values

 + ★ = 6

■ and ★ are variables.
They can have many values,
e.g. ■ = 1 and ★ = 5 or
■ = 4 and ★ = 2.

Venn diagram
- a diagram using intersecting circles or other shapes to show the relationship between sets

vertex
- the point where two or more straight lines meet

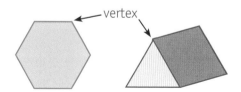

vertex

vertical
- at right angles to the horizon

The tree trunks are vertical.

volume
- the amount of space an object occupies

Volume = 2 x 2 x 2
= 8 cubic units

Units of volume:
cubic centimeters (cm³)
cubic meters (m³)
cubic feet (ft³)

W

week
- a time period of seven days

- Sunday, Monday, Tuesday, Wednesday, Thursday, Friday, Saturday

weight
- the heaviness of an object

Sweets are often sold by weight.

whole
- all of something

- a whole number does not include a fraction or decimal

width
- how wide something is

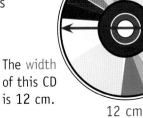

The width of this CD is 12 cm.

12 cm

winter
- the season that follows autumn

x
- the letter that is often used in algebra to stand for an unknown number

x-axis
- the horizontal axis of a graph

x-coordinate
- the position of a point with respect to the x-axis

yard (yd)
- a standard unit of measurement

- equivalent to 3 feet

y-axis
-the vertical axis of a graph

y-coordinate
- the position of a point with respect to the y-axis

year
- a time period of 12 months

- has 365 days in a normal year and 366 days in a leap year

Each new year starts on 1st January.

zero
- a place keeper

- has no value

0

Symbols

$+$	add		π	pi (≈ 3.14)
$-$	subtract		$\circ$	degree
$\times$	multiply		$^\circ C$	degree Celsius
$\div$	divide		$^\circ F$	degree Fahrenheit
			∞	infinity

$<$	less than		$\leftrightarrow$	line
$>$	more than		$\perp$	perpendicular to
$\leq$	less than or equal to		∟	right angle
$\geq$	more than or equal to			parallel lines
$=$	equal to			lines of equal length
$\neq$	not equal to			
$\approx$	approximately equal to			
$\therefore$	therefore			

brackets

( )	parentheses
[ ]	square brackets
{ }	braces

^{2}	(7^2) squared
^{3}	(7^3) cubed
$\sqrt{}$	square root
$\sqrt[3]{}$	cube root

%	percent
.	(6.4) decimal point

Abbreviations

mm	millimeter		g	gram
cm	centimeter		kg	kilogram
m	meter		t	tonne
km	kilometer			
mm^2	square millimeter		oz	ounce
cm^2	square centimeter		lb	pound
m^2	square meter		T	ton
km^2	square kilometer			
cm^3	cubic centimeter		mL	milliliter
m^3	cubic meter		L	liter
			kL	kiloliter
in.	inch			
ft	foot		fl oz	fluid ounce
yd	yard		c.	cup
mi	mile		pt	pint
$in.^2$	square inch		qt	quart
ft^2	square foot		gal	gallon
yd^2	square yard			
$in.^3$	cubic inch		A.M.	anti meridiem (morning)
			P.M.	post meridiem (afternoon or evening)

Equivalent Fraction/Decimal/Percentage Table

Fraction	Decimal	Percentage
$\frac{1}{2}$	0.5	50%
$\frac{1}{3}$	$0.3\overline{3}$	$33\frac{1}{3}\%$
$\frac{1}{4}$	0.25	25%
$\frac{3}{4}$	0.75	75%
$\frac{1}{5}$	0.2	20%
$\frac{2}{5}$	0.4	40%
$\frac{3}{5}$	0.6	60%
$\frac{4}{5}$	0.8	80%
$\frac{1}{8}$	0.125	$12\frac{1}{2}\%$
$\frac{3}{8}$	0.375	$37\frac{1}{2}\%$
$\frac{1}{10}$	0.1	10%
$\frac{1}{20}$	0.05	5%
$\frac{1}{100}$	0.01	1%

Roman numerals

I	= 1	VI	= 6
II	= 2	VII	= 7
III	= 3	VIII	= 8
IV	= 4	IX	= 9
V	= 5	X	= 10

X	= 10	LX	= 60
XX	= 20	LXX	= 70
XXX	= 30	LXXX	= 80
XL	= 40	XC	= 90
L	= 50	C	= 100

C	= 100	DC	= 600
CC	= 200	DCC	= 700
CCC	= 300	DCCC	= 800
CD	= 400	CM	= 900
D	= 500	M	= 1,000

Measurement

Length

10 mm = 1 cm

100 cm = 1 m

1,000 m = 1 km

12 in. = 1 ft

3 ft = 1 yd

1,760 yd = 1 mi

Mass

1,000 g = 1 kg

1,000 kg = 1 t

16 oz = 1 lb

2,000 lb = 1 T

Capacity

1,000 mL = 1 L

1,000 L = 1 kL

8 fl oz = 1 c.

2 c. = 1 pt

2 pt = 1 qt

4 qt = 1 gal

Area

$100 \text{ mm}^2 = 1 \text{ cm}^2$

$10,000 \text{ cm}^2 = 1 \text{ m}^2$

Time

60 seconds = 1 minute

60 minutes = 1 hour

24 hours = 1 day

7 days = 1 week

365 days = 1 year

366 days = 1 leap year

12 months = 1 year

10 years = 1 decade

100 years = 1 century

1,000 years = 1 millennium

Days in a month

September, April, June, and November have 30 days. January, March, May, July, August, October, and December have 31 days. February has 28 days in most years and 29 days in a leap year.

Conversion tables

Converting from standard units of measure to metric units of measure and vice versa (correct to two decimal places)

Length

Standard to Metric

1 inch	2.54 centimeters
1 foot	30.48 centimeters
1 yard	0.91 meters
1 mile	1.61 kilometers

Metric to Standard

1 centimeter	0.39 inch
1 meter	1.09 yard
1 kilometer	0.62 mile

Capacity

Standard to Metric

1 fluid ounce	28.41 milliliters
1 pint	0.57 liter
1 gallon	4.55 liters

Metric to Standard

1 liter	1.76 pints

Mass

Standard to Metric

1 ounce	28.35 grams
1 pound	0.45 kilogram
1 ton	1.02 tonne

Metric to Standard

1 gram	0.04 ounce
1 kilogram	2.20 pounds
1 tonne	0.98 ton

Polygons

Regular polygons

triangle has 3 sides

quadrilateral has 4 sides

pentagon has 5 sides

hexagon has 6 sides

heptagon has 7 sides

octagon has 8 sides

nonagon has 9 sides

decagon has 10 sides

Special quadrilaterals

square
– all sides equal
– all angles equal

rectangle
– opposite sides
  equal
– all angles right angles

rhombus
– all sides equal
– opposite sides
  parallel
– opposite angles equal

parallelogram
– opposite sides
  equal and parallel
– opposite angles
  equal

trapezoid
– one pair of opposite
  sides parallel

kite
– two pairs of equal,
  adjacent sides

Parts of a circle

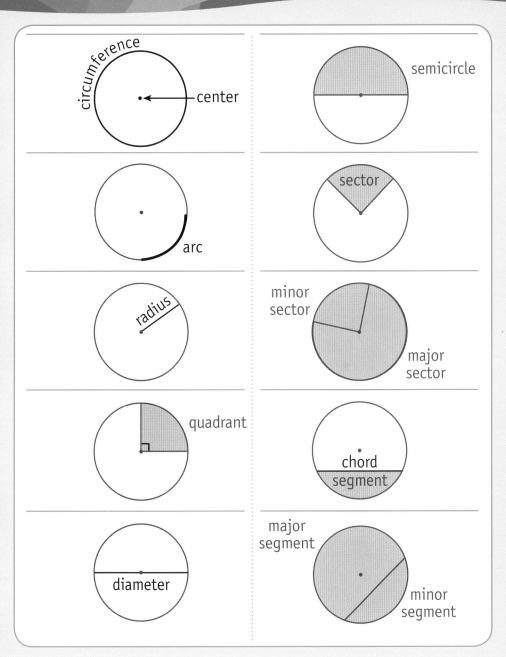

circumference

center

arc

radius

quadrant

diameter

semicircle

sector

minor sector

major sector

chord

segment

major segment

minor segment

Angles

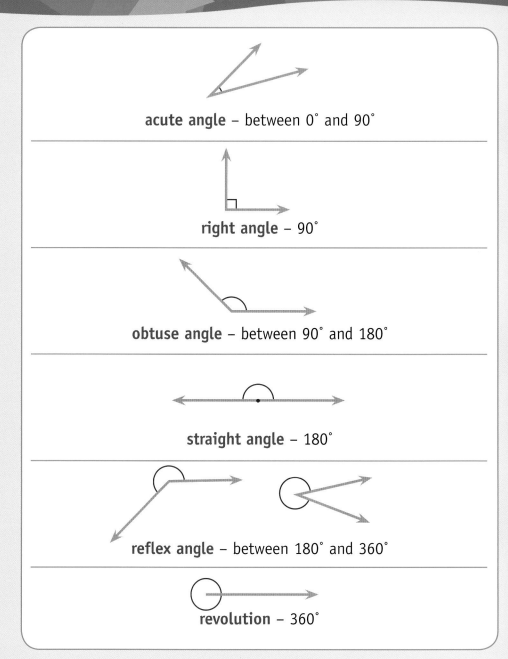

acute angle – between 0° and 90°

right angle – 90°

obtuse angle – between 90° and 180°

straight angle – 180°

reflex angle – between 180° and 360°

revolution – 360°

Triangles

Scalene triangle
- all sides are different lengths
- all angles are different sizes

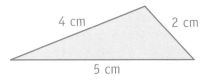

Isosceles triangle
- two sides are equal lengths
- the angles opposite the equal sides are equal in size

Equilateral triangle
- all sides are equal lengths
- all angles are equal in size (60°)

Right triangle
- one angle is a right angle

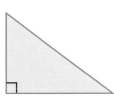

Angle sum
- the three angles always total 180°

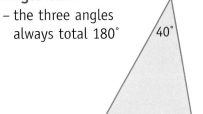

Hypotenuse
- is the side opposite the right angle

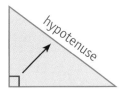

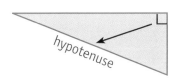

3D objects

 sphere

 cone

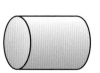 cylinder

 hemisphere

 cube

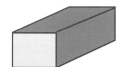 rectangular prism

 triangular prism

 hexagonal prism

 triangular pyramid

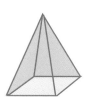 square pyramid

 pentagonal pyramid

 rectangular pyramid

Squared and cubed numbers

Squares	Square roots
$1^2 = 1$	$\sqrt{1} = 1$
$2^2 = 4$	$\sqrt{4} = 2$
$3^2 = 9$	$\sqrt{9} = 3$
$4^2 = 16$	$\sqrt{16} = 4$
$5^2 = 25$	$\sqrt{25} = 5$
$6^2 = 36$	$\sqrt{36} = 6$
$7^2 = 49$	$\sqrt{49} = 7$
$8^2 = 64$	$\sqrt{64} = 8$
$9^2 = 81$	$\sqrt{81} = 9$
$10^2 = 100$	$\sqrt{100} = 10$

Cubes	Cube roots
$1^3 = 1$	$\sqrt[3]{1} = 1$
$2^3 = 8$	$\sqrt[3]{8} = 2$
$3^3 = 27$	$\sqrt[3]{27} = 3$
$4^3 = 64$	$\sqrt[3]{64} = 4$
$5^3 = 125$	$\sqrt[3]{125} = 5$
$6^3 = 216$	$\sqrt[3]{216} = 6$
$7^3 = 343$	$\sqrt[3]{343} = 7$
$8^3 = 512$	$\sqrt[3]{512} = 8$
$9^3 = 729$	$\sqrt[3]{729} = 9$
$10^3 = 1,000$	$\sqrt[3]{1,000} = 10$

Prime numbers to 100

1	2	3	4	5	6	7	8	9	10
11	12	13	14	15	16	17	18	19	20
21	22	23	24	25	26	27	28	29	30
31	32	33	34	35	36	37	38	39	40
41	42	43	44	45	46	47	48	49	50
51	52	53	54	55	56	57	58	59	60
61	62	63	64	65	66	67	68	69	70
71	72	73	74	75	76	77	78	79	80
81	82	83	84	85	86	87	88	89	90
91	92	93	94	95	96	97	98	99	100